A PLUME BOOK

CATALOG LIVING AT ITS MOST ABSURD

Credit: Bridge Mahalik

Molly Erdman is a writer, actor, and comedian based in Los Angeles. She spent eleven years in Chicago, where she was a member of the famed Second City comedy troupe, writing and performing in three Mainstage revues.

Catalog Living
at Its Most Absurd

DECORATING TAKES (WICKER) BALLS

Molly Erdman

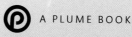

A PLUME BOOK

PLUME
Published by the Penguin Group
Penguin Group (USA) Inc., 375 Hudson Street, New York, New York 10014, U.S.A. • Penguin Group (Canada), 90 Eglinton Avenue East, Suite 700, Toronto, Ontario, Canada M4P 2Y3 (a division of Pearson Penguin Canada Inc.) • Penguin Books Ltd., 80 Strand, London WC2R 0RL, England • Penguin Ireland, 25 St. Stephen's Green, Dublin 2, Ireland (a division of Penguin Books Ltd.) • Penguin Group (Australia), 250 Camberwell Road, Camberwell, Victoria 3124, Australia (a division of Pearson Australia Group Pty. Ltd.) • Penguin Books India Pvt. Ltd., 11 Community Centre, Panchsheel Park, New Delhi – 110 017, India • Penguin Group (NZ), 67 Apollo Drive, Rosedale, Auckland 0632, New Zealand (a division of Pearson New Zealand Ltd.) • Penguin Books (South Africa) (Pty.) Ltd., 24 Sturdee Avenue, Rosebank, Johannesburg 2196, South Africa

Penguin Books Ltd., Registered Offices: 80 Strand, London WC2R 0RL, England

First published by Plume, a member of Penguin Group (USA) Inc.

First Printing, July 2012
10 9 8 7 6 5 4 3 2 1

 REGISTERED TRADEMARK–MARCA REGISTRADA

LIBRARY OF CONGRESS CATALOGING-IN-PUBLICATION DATA
Erdman, Molly.
Catalog living at its most absurd : decorating takes (wicker) balls / Molly Erdman.
p.   cm.
ISBN 978-0-452-29781-4
1. Conduct of life—Humor. 2. Interior decoration—Humor. 3. House furnishings—Humor.
4. Home ownership—Humor. I. Title.
PN6231.C6142E65 2012
818'.602—dc23   2011045773

Printed in the United States of America
Set in Diverda Serif Com with Mundo Sans Std and Walbaum MT Std
Designed by Daniel Lagin

ALWAYS LEARNING   PEARSON

Contents

Acknowledgments

have loads of gratitude first and foremost to Catalog Living's online followers whose support and general lack of mean comments has been an unexpected delight. Thanks to my editor, Nadia Kashper, and everyone at Plume; my agent, Hannah Brown Gordon at Foundry; and my manager, Sam Saifer.

This book would not have been possible without the help of some generous, good-humored folks in the catalog world: Karen Pfaff at Bernard Christianson; Bobbie Renshaw, Emily Brooks, and Christine Dagile at the Source Collection; J. D. Spaulding at Bloomingville; and Jenna Kropp and Sheila Howell at Improvements. Thanks also to Sarah Firshein at Curbed.com, and to everyone behind the scenes at catalog companies who have e-mailed me with contacts, advice, and words of encouragement.

Mom, Dad, Helen, Paul, Emily, Brent, Sofia, and all of my extended family and friends, thank you for your constant encouragement and enthusiasm, not just for this undertaking but for everything.

And, finally, Joe, I couldn't do it without you. Well I suppose I could, but I'd rather not. Thanks for your patience and for laughing at me, usually in a good way.

Oh, and thanks to that one place for not giving me that job I really wanted, because I wouldn't have started the blog if I'd gotten it.

Introduction

Welcome to our home! When the lovely and talented but often underappreciated Molly Erdman told us she wanted to feature our home in her book, we couldn't have been more flattered or surprised. Gary and I never set out to have the rooms of our house featured in any medium—although about three years ago we came very close to having a Swiffer WetJet commercial filmed in one of our third-floor kitchens. Regardless, we're simply thrilled to have the opportunity to show off our home, as well as give you some advice on how to achieve many of the looks seen in this book.

When we first found out about Molly's Catalog Living blog, we were shocked, primarily because all of our computers at home are nonfunctioning Proptronics. A friend of Gary's brought his laptop over to show us the Web site, and imagine our surprise when images appeared on a computer screen! Our next reaction was anger, but that was because Gary's friend knocked a decorative life preserver off the wall. We then became excited once we saw that the blog had a picture of the room with the life preserver still on the wall, so we knew how to put it back. What a great Web site! And now here we are, being featured in a book. One that will hopefully be published in a neutral color to complement any décor.

I am well aware that Gary and I are fortunate to have very high-paying vague jobs, and therefore a larger house than most people. But bear in mind that with great real estate comes great responsibility. Keeping our home perfectly decorated and seasonally appropriate is a year-round job in itself. We start going room by room in September, switching from seashells to gourds, and by the time we get the last one swapped out, it's time to ditch those pumpkins for mini Douglas firs. Our decorating job is never done, providing us with endless challenges and, yes, occasional disagreements.

Your space may not be as large as ours, but that shouldn't stop you from putting all of your time and money into home décor. Taking pride in your home is the most important thing in the world. You could say that family is more important, but it isn't. When you die, people aren't going to care what your career was or if your children went to college. They're going to remember the way you folded dinner napkins into whimsical origami meerkats, that you had your luxurious pima cotton guest towels monogrammed with your guests' initials, and that the food you served matched your wall color.

We hope you enjoy your journey through our home and the invaluable advice we have and are inspired to embark on your own interior design projects. And if those projects feel like they're taking too long, hang up a couple of decorative, nonfunctioning clocks and you'll never know how much of your life you're wasting.

—Elaine

Catalog Living at Its Most Absurd

Chapter 1
THE LIVING ROOM

Although Elaine and I feel strongly about the distinction, for the purposes of this book the terms "living room," "den," "family room," "salon," and "hangin' zone" shall be used interchangeably. Certainly each has nuanced differences, but if you're reading this book you may very well be a novice in the art of room designation, unlike Elaine who teaches a Learning Annex course on it ("When Is It a Mudroom and Not Just an Entryway?" Course #22-4395-01). The term "living room" is yet another example of how words change when passed down through generations; in colonial times, such a space was called a "leaving room" because it was where guests often got into arguments with their hosts and were asked to leave.

Today, the tradition remains. Friendships have been put to the test in a room that witnesses everything from heated games of Chutes and Ladders to suggestions that your friend's religion is fictional. But living rooms have also become a central congregating space for the family, aided by a constant rotation of snacks on the coffee table. Families enjoy kicking back in front of a roaring fire (preferably burning in a fireplace, but a disturbing amount of candles placed around the room will also work), watching television, and staring at, but never reading, books of coordinating hues. In fact—and I would say "ironically" if Elaine wasn't always telling me I use that word incorrectly—living rooms are less about living and more about doing as little as possible. It's a place you can go when you're tired of living and just need to take a break.

There are several strategies you can employ to make your living room a relaxing and cozy retreat. The first thing to address is your television. Displaying a television is a lot like wearing a wedding ring: some people show theirs off, while others pretend it doesn't exist. Should you choose to display your television, consider mounting it on the wall and surrounding it with artwork in hopes of fooling people into thinking it's actually a very abstract piece by the famous artist Samsung. However, if you want to make sure your visitors believe that you actually spend your leisure time reading presidential biographies and listening to NPR, an elegant entertainment armoire is one way to go. If a visitor points to the armoire and asks, "What's in there?" don't panic, simply answer, "The bodies of guests who ask too many questions." Then mention something Terry Gross said in an interview the other day and take a sip of your Yerba Mate.

Much like other rooms in your home, the key to a successful living room lies in the details. Plants are always a wise addition, because they absorb that pesky carbon dioxide that science propagandists claim we emit, and because they offer proof that you are capable of keeping something alive. If you prefer to cheat your way through life and your décor is no exception, there are endless fake plant options, the most popular of which is the Tall Wavy Twig (*Stickus malformidus*), which can be found jutting out of vases in dozens of our rooms. Tall Wavy Twigs bring the eye up, making the room look bigger, as well as making your guests look ridiculous for letting a twig dictate where they look.

Most important, remember that while a living room should be welcoming and relaxing, it should also evoke curiosity. There's no better way to start a conversation than by asking: Why is there a pile of rocks in the corner? How many pillows do you really need on that chair? Where did you find so many apples when they're out of season? If you or your guests are asking these questions, you're doing something right.

Gary, tonight's the kind of night I just want to settle down on the couch with a nice white, taupe, or ecru book.

Elaine, I know I said I'd gather more firewood, but for the life of me I don't know where I put my snowshoes.

Fingers crossed Elaine won't discover that one of her wicker balls is in the neighbor's pool before I can replace it.

Gary, the Fullers will be here any minute! Did you evenly line up the apples on the coffee table yet?

I don't know how they do it, Elaine, but those plants must really want to go upstairs.

Elaine, I know you think it's a fire hazard to light the candles on the wicker table, but don't worry. I have a rolled-up towel nearby for safety.

Gary, how many more times do you think you're going to lick the wall before you believe that it's not candy?

"In some water, in a vase"? Elaine, I could have sworn you said to put the flowers "near the fire, on a plate."

The effervescent hiss of pink champagne, my favorite insect pillow . . . Elaine, I do believe you're trying to seduce me.

If there's one thing I know, it's not to disturb Elaine before she's had her morning coffee and read through her stack of nameless books.

Gary, dinner's ready! Stop playing with your polyhedrons and get up here!

Gary, you can paint over them if you want, but please stop saying you want to "deflower the living room."

It's sad, Elaine. That horse has come so far, but the shiny red sphere has just proven to be an insurmountable obstacle.

Elaine, is it so wrong for me to want just half an hour of time to myself in my Revolutionary War nook?

You were right, Gary. The rusted aluminum siding you found really does provide a great balance to our tiny rock wall.

Decorative schmecorative. Let's face it, Elaine, that dish would hold a lot more fruit than these wimpy little things.

Gary, snake charming happens outside only!

Sure, the sofa is comfortable, Elaine, but I thought it would be romantic to snuggle up on this bath rug with some champagne and a handful of nondescript hardcover books.

Half past Z?! Elaine, I asked you to tell me when it was a quarter to Y!

Gary, are the windows closed? The throw pillows are trying to escape again.

I don't understand. The invitations for the séance clearly said 11:30.

Elaine, I figured out why the plant looked odd. We forgot to put some shells and spheres around it.

Wow. Elaine got up and left her slippers behind; she must have spotted something not off-white in the room and panicked.

Chapter 2
THE BEDROOM

Gary and I take pride in making each one of our bedrooms a relaxing, luxurious, occasionally romantic oasis, whether it's for us or for our cherished guests. It's common knowledge that humans spend five-eighths of their lives in bed, so it's of the utmost importance that we surround ourselves with beauty and function during that large chunk of time.

What makes a good bedroom? First and foremost, of course, is a comfortable bed. Gary and I recommend at least twelve pillows of assorted sizes to provide the necessary head, neck, shoulder, lumbar, and lower-leg support while you sleep. Even in the warm summer months, your body temperature drops as you sleep—about twenty degrees I believe—so plenty of blankets are crucial. We like to layer a cotton sheet, then a flannel sheet, a handmade-looking quilt, a luxurious down comforter, and then finish it off with a cozy chenille throw at the foot of the bed. Now, we realize that all these layers and pillows can complicate your attempt to make the bed to crisp perfection every morning. When you know you need to be out the door in a hurry the next day, we recommend sleeping on the floor.

Bedside tables provide a functional purpose in the bedroom, but don't get caught in the trap of thinking that the only things that belong on them are lamps, alarm clocks, and eczema cream. Bedside tables should be treated like any other flat surface in your home, generously topped with frames with or without photographs, vases with or without flowers, seasonally appropriate trinkets, and, of course, bowls of fruit.

When choosing a color for your bedroom, keep in mind the old saying "Having too many colors in your bedroom leads to night terrors." What colors are best for a bedroom, you ask? I'm sure you'll be relieved to know that bedrooms no longer require soothing colors like sea grass, summer wheat, and prairie sky. Just as it's acceptable these days to break previously held fashion rules like not wearing purple before Columbus Day, it's also acceptable to disregard research indicating that colors like yellow and orange make people restless. Bottom line, as long as you have a nightgown to match it, any color can be a bedroom color.

There are other little touches you can provide to take your bedroom to the next level. No one can deny the allure of breakfast in bed, but equally undeniable is the risk of food and beverage stains. Eliminate this risk by serving your guests or spouse the *idea* of breakfast in bed, as demonstrated by a tray of empty coffee cups, a stylish decanter, and/or thick-skinned, leak-free fruit. This tray, remarkably, serves as both a kind gesture and a passive-aggressive indication that it's time to get up.

Hopefully, these tips will help transform your bedroom from a place you hide when guests are around, quickly shutting the door, shielding it with your body, and screaming "Don't go in there!" to a tranquil retreat that you're so proud of you're constantly asking your visitors, "May I show you my bedroom?"

You just never know these days if your guests are going to have a strong preference for gray or taupe, so it's just best to have both available.

Elaine, I'm exhausted. I just want to get in bed and watch the back of the TV.

Gary, that is by no means what I meant by a feather bed.

Elaine and I were going for that "sleeping outside while staring at a giant bowling pin" feel.

Gary, check the book again because I'm pretty sure the whole point of the trick is to keep the plate of pears on the bed.

You say "it looks like an old woman melted on the chair" like it's a bad thing, **Gary.**

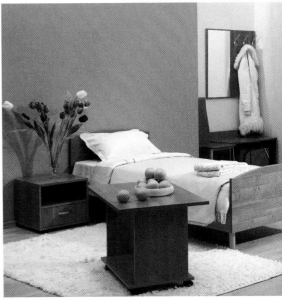

I know it's late, but how about some light reading and a couple goblets of mead before bed?

Elaine, I'm much too tired. Wheel the fruit table to the bedside, would you?

I think I know just the dress to wear when I mow the headboard today.

Your topiary hobby has crossed a line, **Gary.**

Gary, I told you they weren't marshmallows, and I'm sorry you feel your pride won't allow you to spit them out.

Hard-boiling those condor eggs before we went to bed last night was one of your best ideas in a long time, **Gary.**

Elaine, have you considered that perhaps your "encouraging" wallpaper choice is only putting more pressure on me?

No, Gary, when life gives you lemons, *you* have to make lemonade.

Almost ready! My hat just needs to finish warming.

Elaine, if you don't get rid of the acoustically challenging wheat sheaves, I can no longer be expected to provide your morning serenades.

Were you eating peanuts in here, Gary? The ceiling broke out in hives again.

Yes, Gary, it's a lovely photo of your niece. Don't you think we could find a better spot for it?

It's a nice gesture, Gary, but it won't make up for your ridiculous demand for a minimalist bedroom.

Elaine, I have no idea what you're talking about. What hint that you wanted to go to the beach?

Drat! Slept through my apple alarm again, Elaine. Now I have to rush to eat all of them before work.

I'm not sure I want to know why there are four teacups on our bedtime tea tray, **Gary.**

Old-timey traveling salesman fantasy again, **Elaine?**

What? No! I definitely wasn't wearing a woman's camisole and spying on the neighbors. Why do you ask, **Elaine?**

That's the last time the Clarks stay with us. They stole one of our orbs and didn't even accept the welcome cactus we gave them!

Chapter 3
THE KITCHEN
& DINING ROOM

Many people say the kitchen is the heart of the home, but what idiot wouldn't think to call it the stomach of the home?

Now, I know what you're expecting. I'm going to tell you that I don't know anything about the kitchen because Elaine does all the cooking, right? Wrong. I actually fancy myself a bit of a chef, although I do not fancy using the word "fancy" as a verb. Cooking is an excellent activity for couples to partake in together, since the kitchen offers many readily available weapons should an argument erupt.

The kitchen is a utilitarian room, and its décor is most easily created from common items you already have. Bowls of fruit are, of course, appropriate for any room in the house but are perhaps a bit too obvious a choice for the kitchen. Instead of using a bowl, unleash your produce and consider patterned counter displays. Branch out and explore nonfruit items to show off, such as vegetables, nuts, and deli meat.

In order to make your kitchen the showpiece it deserves to be, it is crucial to have as much counter space as possible. This is achieved by keeping everything tucked away in spacious cabinets. While our upper cabinets have a standard depth of twelve inches, our bottom cabinets lead into a four-hundred-square-foot secret kitchen storage room. So if you see Elaine or me crawling into our bottom kitchen cabinets, that's most likely where we're going.

Your family probably eats their meals huddled over the kitchen sink, but Elaine and I believe that if you're going to put the time and effort into cooking, you should have a dining space worthy of such a venture. Ornate, formal place settings create the mood for a delicious meal, and you should consider what you're going to be eating when deciding on dishware and table decoration. Do some research into the history of the dish being prepared, and see if you can special order plates or utensils from the country of origin. Elaine and I understand that in these hectic times, not everyone can go to that much trouble, so just go with your best guess and assume that it will only be marginally offensive. Ideally, however, setting the table should take as long as cooking the meal.

Lighting is a critical and often overlooked part of any dining experience. Good lighting can be the difference in your mashed potatoes looking like wall Spackle or looking like something you wouldn't want to eat. A chandelier above your table can add drama, both in its design and in the knowledge that at any minute it could come crashing down into your pot roast. Light a few candles, and not only will it score some romance points with the wife, it will also provide a handy heat source if that chicken is a little too pink for your comfort level.

So stop shoveling Lean Cuisines down your gullet while watching television. You might get the couch dirty and be punished with gourd-polishing duty for the next five years. Instead, consider making your meals a meaningful shared experience for you and your family. Or, at the very least, make your kitchen and dining room look like you care about that sort of thing.

I know you asked me to make dinner, Elaine, but it's nearly impossible to roast a chicken with those guys staring down at me.

Decorative or not, Gary, I can't help but be insulted when you insist on having a trash can next to you when you eat my cooking.

I do like it, Gary. I just don't know if steak night was the best time to break out the new rug.

Bad news, Elaine. Since their last battle, the bok choy have brought in some reinforcements against the apples.

No, I'm not scared, Elaine. I'm just not in a pistachio mood this evening, if you must know.

Kids, run for it. Your mom has her sarcastic wall art up again.

Elaine, perhaps the reason I don't cook more often is because you find the need to have angels watching over you when you eat my food.

Let's see . . . frying, broiling, baking . . . Gary, where's my sautéing hat?

Gary, please put your napkin back in your lap.

Do you even know what "rewiring the chandelier" means, **Gary?**

Great news, Elaine. I found another portion of a brown paper bag I'd like to frame.

The plate must have smelled your brisket and decided to jump, **Elaine.**

Twelve-thirty is the actual time.
The other time is a little something
we call **"Gary Standard Time."**

Oh, perfect. Elaine, you knew I was planning to wear my red vest and black bow tie.

Gary's in another one of his paranoid phases. Now I have to squeeze lemon juice on his grocery list and hold it over a flame to find out what we need at the store.

Whenever Gary's mother comes to visit, he goes on a kitchen cleaning spree and turns slightly British.

I'm happy to do the dishes, Elaine, as long as I can have my art supplies, coins, and favorite set of combs where I can see them.

Elaine, do you have the receipt? There was one apple in the batch that weighs nothing.

No, Gary, I'll show you one more time. It goes wicker place mat, brown charger, white plate, rolled napkin, nubby wooden sphere, and then napkin stuffed in wineglass.

Elaine, I'm not going to lie to you. This new cereal is not my favorite.

Gary, when you said you wanted to bring something to the table, I didn't think you meant it literally and I certainly didn't think you meant a different chair from everyone else.

Elaine, now can I turn on
the air conditioner?

Chapter 4
THE BATHROOM

While most people will go to great lengths to personalize their homes, bathrooms tend to get neglected when it comes to décor. Yes, bathrooms are functional rooms, but that doesn't mean they can't be beautiful as well. Research shows that we spend five hours a day in the bathroom, so Gary and I can't imagine why anyone would spend all that time looking at ordinary plastic shower curtain rings and non-custom-designed toothpaste tubes.

The first important aspect of making the most of your bathroom is to stop relegating this important room to such a tiny space. Consider converting one of your lesser-used bedrooms into a bathroom, or building an addition to your house to create more space. Many people think a bathroom consists of just a sink, a toilet, and a bathtub and/or shower, but those people make us very sad. Why not add a comfortable upholstered chair to sit in after your shower? Or bring the outdoors in with what some may consider an alarming number of plants?

Organization is critical to a successful bathroom. Keeping only one color of towels eliminates guesswork and color wheel consultation. Keep them folded or rolled up in wicker baskets, preferably labeled "Towels" to prevent someone (Gary) from confusing them with flour tortillas and using them to make inedible but absorbent quesadillas. Countertops should be free of clutter, and, ideally, free of anything at all (with the possible exception of a nautical-shaped soap and a color-coordinated towel). Everyone knows that items like seashells, oars, and starfish will help remind people that they're in a room where water is a prominent feature, and dozens of candles will add a surprising pop of fire. Rubber "duckies" provide the nearly impossible-to-achieve balance of whimsy and creepiness.

Many items used to decorate other rooms of your house are also appropriate in the bathroom, but you need to make sure they can withstand getting wet. To do this, simply toss your favorite vase, wicker ball, or antlers in a full bathtub. Wait thirty seconds, and whatever isn't warped or disintegrated is safe for bathroom adornment. If you're still itching to use a water-sensitive item in your bathroom, no problem! Just move it to your designated "display" bathroom and, to be safe, disconnect all plumbing from this room and glue the toilet seat down (thanks to Gary for providing the necessity for this last tip).

Many people are bothered by the wasted space created by an empty bathtub. Take advantage of this opportunity to unexpectedly dazzle your visitors by filling your tub with sea glass, throw pillows, or a life-size mannequin wearing a life preserver. When you want to take a bath, simply dispose of the decorative elements by flushing them down the toilet.

Speaking of toilets, do everything in your power to avoid them being seen. Create a separate toilet closet off the main bathroom for privacy, or at the very least cover it with a rattan hamper when not in use. Much like a car's engine is tucked away in the trunk, the "motor" of the bathroom should be similarly concealed. Make your bathroom a place you and your guests want to tell everyone they've just visited!

Let me save you some heartache, Elaine. These bathtub strawberries taste terrible.

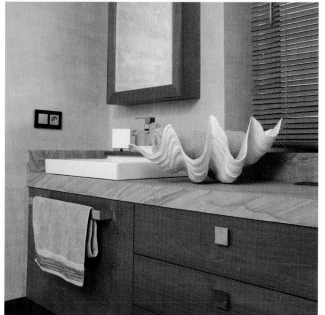

It's impressive, Gary, but you know I've repeatedly asked you to clean your giant shells outside.

Gary! We've got faucet weeds again!

Today's one of those days when I just like to curl up with a cup of coffee and a good book in a dry, cold bathtub.

I don't know, Elaine. Am I feeling the Sink of Good or the Sink of Evil this morning?

Oh, washroom! For a second there, Elaine, I assumed I was in the woods, holding my hands into a narrow but forceful waterfall.

Gary, I've asked you dozens of times to please use floss and not our decorative bamboo twigs.

Sorry, Elaine, but it's the only alone time I have to practice my juggling.

Did someone have an extra cup of coffee and find the leaf stencil?

Elaine, don't for one second think that someday I won't stand slightly to the left of the designated sink spot.

If you don't have green stalky things sticking out of a shallow bowl of sand, well then you just don't have a bath.

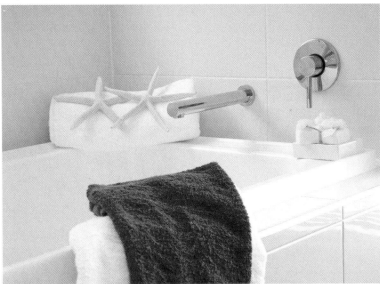

I'm assuming it's not the purpose Elaine intended, but I can't deny that these starfish really do the trick on my heel calluses.

We can wash them and surround them with scented candles and herbs all we want, Elaine, but let's face it, Uncle Joe's B.O. is embedded in our towels for eternity.

Gary, it's been a long day, and I'd just like to soak in a tub with some moss balls, aerosol cans, and a large tree's worth of firewood.

I don't much care for it, but **Gary** claims it helps him live out his childhood fantasy of bathing in the Astrodome.

Oh no, Gary, another loofah face down in the water. No doubt the work of the rival washcloth gang.

If you know something better to do with it, Elaine, you can clean the shower drain next time.

In case someone wants to keep me company during bath time, Elaine. That's why.

I appreciate the gesture, Gary, but frankly I don't know if you're trying to romance me or burn me.

We have the red guest towels, rug, and plant base out, so it goes without saying you should only use bath products in red bottles during your stay.

Elaine, I'm so sorry, I accidentally took a bath in the Clean Bathroom when I was a little dirty.

Come on, Elaine, get in here and tell me if it looks like I have horns when I'm on the toilet.

Elaine, sometimes you gotta scare the duckie a little, just so he appreciates how good he has it.

See, Gary? You didn't gain weight; you just needed to put down the starfish.

Ha ha, Elaine, I get it. I was in the bathroom a long time.

Chapter 5
THE CHILDREN'S ROOMS

An ancient Greek poet once wrote, "I believe the children are our future." Elaine and I believe that to be one of the biggest lies ever told, up there with the existence of Antarctica and the whole high-fructose corn syrup controversy. Children, we believe, are our present, although I regret the unfortunate wordplay that makes this sound like they are also gifts. What we mean is that children keep you in the immediate moment, sucking you into their careless attitudes. Elaine insists that I mean "carefree," but she had her chance to write this chapter intro and she chose to go to her cardio eye-rolling class instead, so what I say goes.

A big problem that comes with having children is storage. Where do you keep them? Whenever possible, we like putting children into an existing room—perhaps one previously used for overnight guests or for starfish storage—rather than building an addition onto the house. The first thing to assess when decorating your child's room is gender. If, like us, you've given your children names like Morgan, Taylor, or Soup, and your wife has suggested that you let them do whatever they want with their hair, you may need to consult their birth certificates to confirm this information. Once you know if you're dealing with a boy or a girl, you can start looking to other aspects of the child's personality for ideas.

Does your child enjoy fun? If so, you may want to consider putting some toys in the room. Stuffed animals, precious miniature versions of various forms of transportation, and rudimentary building materials all fall under the "toy" category. While these items may seem incredibly boring to you, many children are afflicted with a condition called "imagination" and are able to entertain themselves for hours.

Do you have old sports equipment or memorabilia that your wife is politely demanding that you get rid of? Give those treasured items a second life by decorating your child's room with them. Footballs, baseball cards, and your old uniform from the summer you worked at Foot Locker all make excellent decoration for your sports-loving offspring. And if he is not the athletic child you'd hoped for, placing these objects around his room will provide a constant reminder of his shortcoming and possibly inspire him to try something at which he will no doubt fail. If my father hadn't put a cricket bat in my boyhood room, I never would have misheard what it was, and I wouldn't have gone to a meeting of the intramural croquet squad in college where I met Elaine's attractive roommate Sheila. And, eventually, Elaine.

Rooms can be designed to fit a child's essence, but what if that essence is eluding you? It's never too early to assume that your child may not be very bright. If that's the case, consider room decorations that are educational, like letters, numbers, and, if he is particularly forgetful, his name. If your child is reluctant to go to sleep at night, fool him with a bed shaped like something he enjoys, like a race car, castle, or comedic actor Kevin James.

Elaine and I realize that all of this can seem somewhat overwhelming, especially knowing that however you decorate your children's rooms will dictate their level of success in life. If the pressure is too much, keep in mind that it's never too early to get your kids started on beige.

Don't worry, Carter. The lobsters only come out if you're not asleep by nine.

Say what you will, Elaine, but I'm thrilled that Joey's taking up 1970s tennis.

Serving that single giraffe mom and her son with an eviction notice was one of the toughest things I've ever had to do, but Sofia was adamant that they were late-night partiers.

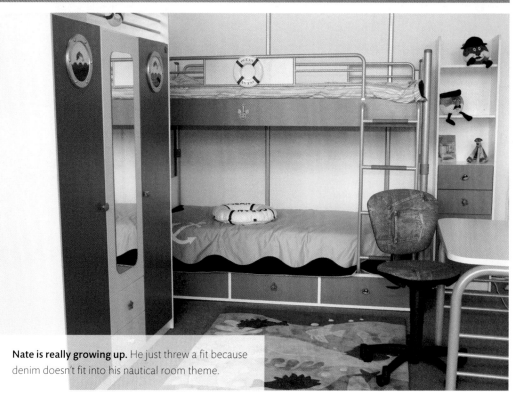

Nate is really growing up. He just threw a fit because denim doesn't fit into his nautical room theme.

Sure, Carson, Mommy and I are sleepy too. But no one's going to bed until you nail three more jump shots and at least one dunk.

I admit, Gary, that maybe we made a mistake naming her, but is this going to happen whenever I ask you to put Thyme to bed?

Look at those blank stares, Gary. I'm afraid Emily's stuffed animals are stupid.

Don't be silly, Lola. The horsies aren't trying to escape from your crib because they're afraid someone will stick a pole through them and ride them.

Ever since we installed this netting over all the kids' beds, our cases of household malaria are down 75 percent.

We don't want to force our kids into thinking there's a "right" order to the alphabet.

Gary Jr. has been afraid to go in his room ever since his robot claimed world domination.

You know, Elaine, I just worry we're not doing enough to ensure she grows up to love purses and shoes.

Gary, I know it might be more effective outside, but this way her bedroom is a tax write-off.

We hung a onesie up that's one size smaller to try to encourage Rosie to drop a couple of pounds before the big party.

Logan, not your best puppet show. Sure, the M&M liked it, but he's always been a little too easy to please.

Elaine, you can't possibly expect me to get Tyler to his art table during rush hour.

We really want Holden to master the midrange single digits before we move on to higher numbers.

**Gary, Zach was born a week ago and the stork is still here.** Did you forget to tip him?

I wanted to erase it, Gary, but Max wanted a reminder of the closest he ever came to winning at tic-tac-toe.

Just like we let him choose a name for himself, we're waiting to let Donut choose a decorating scheme for his room.

Well, Parker, looks like your toys agree with your mother and me that your sister is more fun.

Porter can never get to sleep without her teddy bear, a bucket of starfish, and her unfinished wooden birdhouse.

I don't know, Elaine, is our dig at Grace's bed wetting too subtle?

Chapter 6
OUTDOOR SPACES

The phrase "the great outdoors," coined in the 1988 Dan Aykroyd and John Candy film of the same name, is, of course, an oxymoron. Riddled with bugs, inclement weather, and unflattering natural light, the outside is, Gary and I firmly believe, not fit for human existence. But what happens when we bring out a seven-piece all-weather living room suite and a colorful array of fifteen-foot patio umbrellas? How about a solar-powered wine fridge and a sixty-four-inch flat screen mounted above your outdoor fireplace? Suddenly, this hostile space becomes somewhere you'll proudly call "a place I can comfortably sit."

You already know that Gary and I consider pillows to be one of the most critical design elements inside your house; outside, where jagged sticks, thorny greenery, and fanged animals threaten you constantly, the soft protection of pillows and cushions is especially important. The general rule of thumb for pillow use is that your outdoor cushioning should equal your indoor preference times eleven. You can either invest in outdoor pillows, made with fabric and stuffing that can withstand the elements, or simply toss out your weather-worn pillows on a weekly basis (they're called "throw pillows" for a reason!).

Many people who venture outdoors are tempted to take part in the gardening trend. While Gary and I enjoy the aspect of this activity that says, "I have plenty of time on my hands and money to blow on hand-painted herb name placards," gardening is, by and large, an enormous waste of time. Artificial plants, on the other hand, offer the lush look of a full garden with the added benefit of supporting the plastics industry. Missing the smell of fresh flowers? A solid minute of dousing with your favorite aerosol room spray (or eau de toilette, in a pinch) will fill your yard with the scent of an authentic garden/Polynesian vacation/basket of clean linens.

The good news about the outdoors is that being there warrants the purchase of various accessories. These days no one ventures into the sun without a fashionable straw hat. Even when you're safely indoors, leaving hats strewn randomly around your yard indicates that someone was recently spending time there. Bear in mind, of course, that once your hat touches the ground it should never go back on your head, or you will run the risk of worms burrowing into your skull. It is therefore of the utmost importance to designate your hats for either wearing or display.

To add further evidence to the charade that you participate in backyard activities, you'll need an assortment of yard tools. Popular yard tools include rakes, shovels, and miniature rakes and shovels. Should you find yourself in a situation where a guest asks what a particular tool is for, a safe bet is to respond "aerating the soil," since chances are this is beyond her level of gardening knowledge and she will not press further. These assorted tools, which usually feature some kind of metal, are best left outside at all times. Not only does this avoid the problem of dirt transport (see worm burrowing, above), but it also allows for a lovely patina, sometimes called "rust," to form.

Always keep in mind that your yard is part of your house, and just like any other room, it needs constant care, maintenance, and décor rotation. But with just a few simple steps you can turn your outdoor space into something you can pretend to enjoy up to one-sixth of the year.

What do you mean you couldn't find the tiny grapes on the back porch tchotchke shelf? They're between the sideways mugs and the candy jar plate.

Elaine! The first throw pillow harvest of the season!

I've always loved seeing the tote bags shedding the last of their leaves, signifying that winter is finally here.

Even on a gloomy day like this, nothing beats heading out to the dock, sitting on my favorite stools, and eating shrimp cocktail out of a fishing net.

Gary, I assure you the phrase is not "take a long nap on a short pier."

I don't know, Elaine. I still think I'm at risk for butt splinters.

Oh, Elaine, what makes you think you know more about proper snow removal tools than I do?

Okay, Gary, you win. You're officially relieved from scarecrow-making duty.

Gary, if you look at me with that stupid grin and say "Get it?" one more time, I'll bury you in that flower bed.

You're right, Gary, I can't be mad. I did in fact tell you to "do something with all these pots."

Just give him a minute, Elaine. Looks like he's taking Jake's departure for college the hardest of any of us.

I really hate that one gnome, Elaine. Standing there smoking his pipe while the others gather rabbits in the woods. What nerve.

Elaine, I brought you more tea.
Elaine? ELAINE???

I don't get it, Gary. No matter how beautiful I think our garden is, she looks at it with such disappointment.

On a beautiful day like this, how can you deny your throw pillows a bike ride through the neighborhood?

It's very sweet, Gary, although there's a chance the sign may defeat the purpose.

Well sure, Elaine, when you remove the sheet I can see it's not actually a chair ghost.

Gary, look! The first Adirondack crossing of the season. Majestic.

I don't know how they figured it out, Gary, but the plants have broken into the house.

Playing outside with the herbs is fun for a little while, Elaine, but they always need you to give them another push.

I'm sorry I doubted you, Elaine. This pre-horse show tailgating really does get pretty wild.

Lucky for us, Gary, the best weapon against fake bears is an antler candle holder.

Chapter 7
OTHER SPACES

At this point you've probably been looking through this book, thinking to yourself and shouting to anyone who'll listen, "This is all well and good, but not every space in my house fits into one of your tidy categories, you elitist numbskulls." Elaine and I understand your frustration, which is why we created this final chapter, featuring all those other spaces in your home that you may not have a name for. We, of course, do have names for them, but since one family's "back corridor" is another family's "tertiary hallway," we figured we would use this chapter to encompass them all.

Many people work from home or pretend that they do. What once was called a "study" and was adorned with rich wood bookshelves and leather chairs has given way to the "home office," which usually features a laptop, some orderly stacks of papers and books, and wall art featuring very straightforward objects like a plant or coffee cup. You can liven up this depressing room by bringing in whimsical objects that showcase your personality. Always running late? Putting several clocks on the wall will confuse people. They won't know whether to be angry that you have all these clocks and are still late or to appreciate the fact that you are obviously self-aware. Do you acknowledge that technology is important but still want people to know you're none too pleased about it? An old-fashioned typewriter drives that point home, especially if placed on a high shelf in a way that says, "Back in the day I used this thing."

Elaine and I are always looking for new places in our home to put random assorted items, or as we prefer to call them, "life souvenirs." Hallways, corners, staircases, butler pantries, foyers, antechambers, vestibules, and nooks (though not necessarily crannies) are all spaces just begging to be styled. Make a hallway more than just a depressing tunnel of nothingness by placing a cherished collection of rocks or leaves on a slim console table. Transform your entryway coatrack into something fashionable by insisting that your family and guests all buy coats in the same color family. Help orphaned vases you couldn't find a home for in any other room feel special by tucking them in a dark, isolated corner.

Just as you always wear your nicest, most flattering underwear in case you are stripped down naked in the street by rabid fans, it is in your best interest to decorate the spaces in your home that no one may see for years on end. Thoughtful design in a place rarely seen is the mark of a truly exceptional human being.

My trick to staying fit while working a sedentary job? Hourly walks to my coffee cup.

I have to hand it to you, Elaine. The addition of the oars and fake fish really makes our tribute to Mittens complete.

Of course I've embraced technology, Gary, but there's no reason not to have a quill and ink under glass, just for emergencies.

Whenever Elaine and I are undecided on a work of art, we like to get the opinion of the bowl of oranges.

Gary, I've got to finish this report. Would you please feed the plastic dog and shaggy carpet balls so I can work in peace?

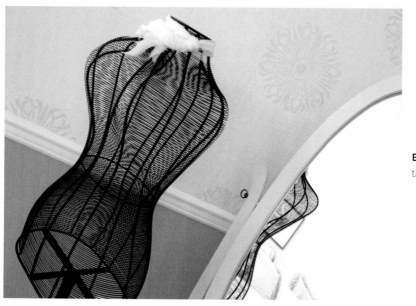

Elaine, you have no idea what it takes to design my line of ascots.

Well, pencil's sharp. Let's call it a day.

Elaine! One of my balls never made it back from the polisher!

Gary, will you hang Hannah's scooter back on the antlers where it belongs?

Ha! Now Elaine will never know I spilled grape juice on the chair. And then moved to the other chair and spilled more grape juice.

Yes, Gary, very funny. Can we agree that you saying "bull's-eye" every time you sit down has run its course?

Now the owl is looking at me funny too. Elaine! Bring me another bell jar!

Please, Elaine. If you're not supposed to put a plant under the nesting tables, they wouldn't make see-through nesting tables!

Eleven-fifty already? Boy, time flies when you shuffle papers and stare longingly at pictures of red wine and a blurry hot babe.

"Time to leave the world"? Your prop-based word games are getting morbid, Gary.

Clocks displaying different time zones, a set of dry-erase boards, a stack of perfectly aligned white books, and a vaseful of breadsticks. Yup, Elaine, I'm ready to start my plan for world domination.

I admit, Gary, I may have taken cleaning off my desk a bit too far.

I just think the sign might seem more genuine if it actually faced the door, **Gary.**

I hate to admit it, Elaine, but I get a real rush depriving things of the water they need to survive.

Lucky for you one of us remembered the gray urn's daffodil allergy before things got messy, **Elaine.**

Seriously, Elaine. With all your jackets, bags, and aprons, you can hardly see our festive holiday coatrack lights.

Go ahead and start dinner, hon.
I just need to pack my violin and schooner into my rattan briefcase.

Gary, I found your favorite piece of green wire. Did you even think to look under your precariously balanced rock arrangement?

You can't bring flowers for one and not the other! Gary, you have a lot to learn about vases' feelings.

Gary, if you keep jumping off the balcony every time you think you see a fish, I'll have no choice but to take the binoculars away.

A Fond Farewell

Gary and I hope you've enjoyed this tour through our house. Now the fun can begin for you, when you embark on your own design journey. Remember, decorating your home is a way to express what makes you who you are, and hopefully we've provided the inspiration to make your home unique just like ours.

You may feel immense pressure after seeing the rooms in our house. This is perfectly normal and appreciated. Just remember, there is no "right" or "wrong" way to create your space, except that there is only one "right" way.

In order to start living like we do, you'll need to start shopping like we do. And since only people who are trying too hard would ever carry a book around with them, we created this handy shopping list to take along as you begin your journey.

GARY AND ELAINE'S HANDY TAKE-ALONG SHOPPING LIST

- ☐ **Starfish** (preferably nonliving)
- ☐ **Shells** (artificial or polished to artificial level)
- ☐ **Wicker balls** (rattan acceptable in a pinch)
- ☐ **Lanterns and candles** (plan on burning three candles per lantern per day)
- ☐ **Limes** (four to five crates per week)
- ☐ **Other fruit** (no pineapple)
- ☐ **Off-white paperback books** (beige, ecru also acceptable in a pinch)
- ☐ **Books in one** (1) other color of your choice
- ☐ **Pillows** (enough for daily rotation)
- ☐ **Vases**
- ☐ **Additional vases**
- ☐ **Tall wavy twigs** (faux or professionally smoothed)
- ☐ **Assorted gourds** (late August through November only)
- ☐ **Rocks** (mix of polished and regular)

(Take to office supply store and ask them to cut here.)

IMAGE CREDITS